Baby Animals in the Wild!

Beaver Kits in the Wild

by Katie Chanez

Ideas for Parents and Teachers

Bullfrog Books let children practice reading informational text at the earliest reading levels. Repetition, familiar words, and photo labels support early readers.

Before Reading

- Discuss the cover photo. What does it tell them?

- Look at the picture glossary together. Read and discuss the words.

Read the Book

- "Walk" through the book and look at the photos. Let the child ask questions. Point out the photo labels.

- Read the book to the child, or have him or her read independently.

After Reading

- Prompt the child to think more. Ask: Beaver kits swim and spend a lot of time in water. Can you name other baby animals that swim?

Bullfrog Books are published by Jump!
5357 Penn Avenue South
Minneapolis, MN 55419
www.jumplibrary.com

Library of Congress Cataloging-in-Publication Data

Names: Chanez, Katie, author.
Title: Beaver kits in the wild / by Katie Chanez.
Description: Minneapolis, MN: Jump!, Inc., [2024]
Series: Baby animals in the wild! | Includes index.
Audience: Ages 5–8
Identifiers: LCCN 2022045876 (print)
LCCN 2022045877 (ebook)
ISBN 9798885244039 (hardcover)
ISBN 9798885244046 (paperback)
ISBN 9798885244053 (ebook)
Subjects: LCSH: Beavers—Infancy—Juvenile literature.
Classification: LCC QL737.R632 C43 2024 (print)
LCC QL737.R632 (ebook)
DDC 599.37/139—dc23/eng/20220930
LC record available at https://lccn.loc.gov/2022045876
LC ebook record available at https://lccn.loc.gov/2022045877

Editor: Eliza Leahy
Designer: Molly Ballanger

Photo Credits: Robert B McGouey/All Canada Photos/SuperStock, cover; KamalaNPS/Shutterstock, 1; JasonOndreicka/iStock, 3; Michael D. Bowen/Shutterstock, 4, 23bm; Zoran Kolundziia/iStock, 5, 23bl; Klaus Brauner/Shutterstock, 6–7; Jody Ann/Shutterstock, 8; Photoshot - NHPA/SuperStock, 9, 23br; Suzi Eszterhas/Minden Pictures/SuperStock, 10–11; Tom Uhlman/Alamy, 12–13, 23tm; Jeff Foott/Minden Pictures/SuperStock, 14; Robert McGouey/Wildlife/Alamy, 15, 22br; stanley45/iStock, 16–17; Dan Pepper/iStock, 18; Matthew H Irvin/iStock, 18–19, 23tr; Bernd Zoller/imageBROKER/SuperStock, 20–21; Stan Tekiela Author/Naturalist/ Wildlife Photographer/Getty, 22 (top); Diane079F/iStock, 22bl; tuuliiumala/Shutterstock, 23tl; Geoffrey Kuchera/Shutterstock, 24.

Printed in the United States of America at Corporate Graphics in North Mankato, Minnesota.

Table of Contents

Teeth and Tails

Look at the pond.

There is a beaver lodge!

lodge

A mom and her kits come out.

kit

They swim.

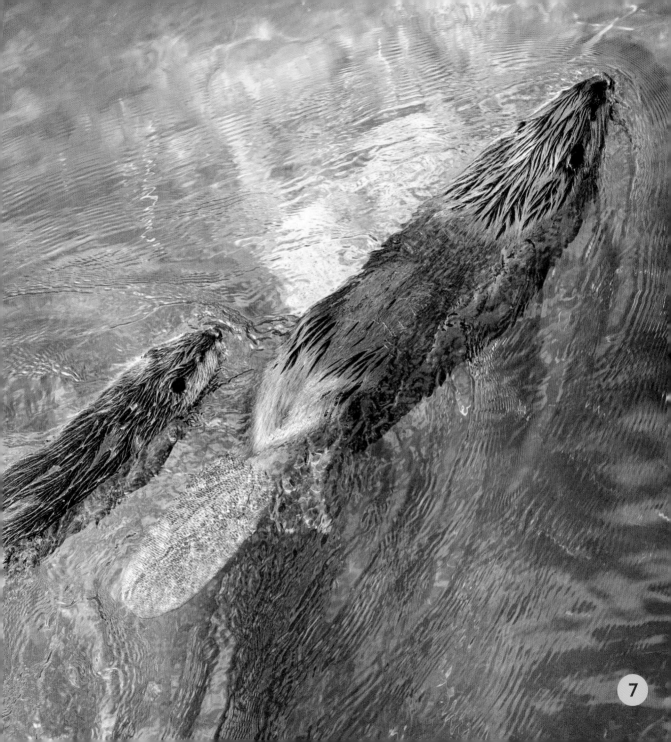

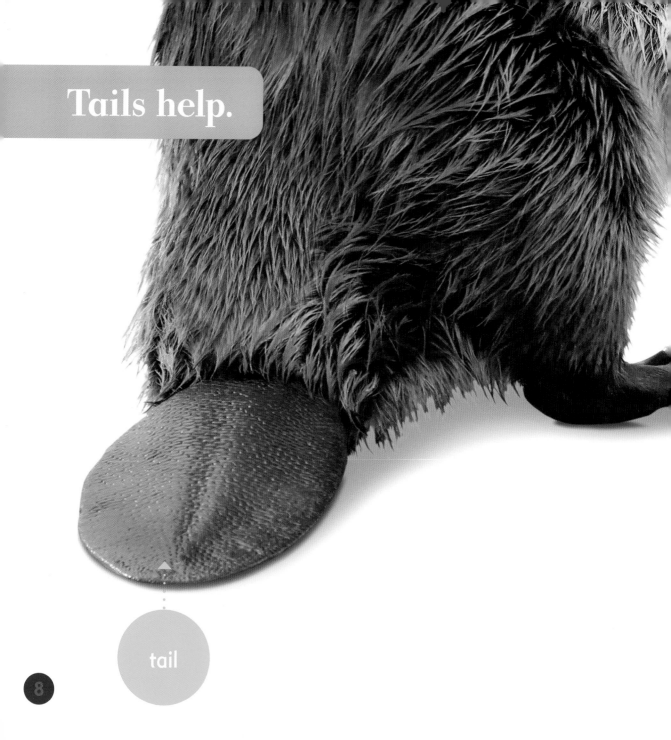

Tails help.

tail

8

So do webs between their toes.

web

They look for food.

They eat leaves and bark.

Mmm!

The kits grow.

They stay with the group.

It is called a colony.

colony

13

They chew wood.
Why?

Their teeth never stop growing! Chewing keeps them short.

tooth

The kits grow up.
They use their teeth
to cut down trees.

One builds a dam.
It uses sticks and mud.
The dam stops water.

dam

Now the beaver can build
its own lodge.

Happy building!

Parts of a Beaver Kit

What are the parts of a beaver kit? Take a look!

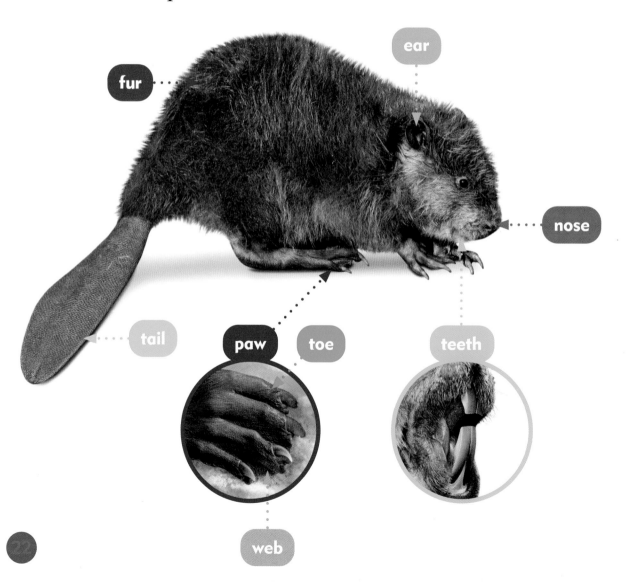

fur

ear

nose

tail

paw

toe

teeth

web

Picture Glossary

bark
The tough outer covering on the stems of trees and other plants.

colony
A group of beavers.

dam
A barrier across a stream or river that holds back water.

kits
Baby beavers.

lodge
The home of a beaver.

webs
The folds of skin that connect the toes of some animals that swim.

Index

To Learn More

Finding more information is as easy as 1, 2, 3.

❶ Go to www.factsurfer.com

❷ Enter "beaverkits" into the search box.

❸ Choose your book to see a list of websites.